SPORTS SCIENCE PROJECTS

WHEELS!

SCIENCE PROJECTS
with BICYCLES, SKATEBOARDS, and SKATES

Madeline Goodstein

Enslow Publishers, Inc.
40 Industrial Road
Box 398
Berkeley Heights, NJ 07922
USA

http://www.enslow.com

Library of Congress Cataloging-in-Publication Data

Goodstein, Madeline P.
   Wheels! science projects with bicycles, skateboards, and skates / Madeline Goodstein.
      p. cm. — (Score! sports science projects)
   Includes bibliographical references and index.
   Summary: "Presents several science experiments and science project ideas using physics and bicycles, skateboards, and roller skates"—Provided by publisher.
   ISBN-13: 978-0-7660-3107-4
   ISBN-10: 0-7660-3107-1
   1. Physics—Experiments—Juvenile literature. 2. Science—Experiments—Juvenile literature. 3. Wheels—Juvenile literature. 4. Science projects—Juvenile literature. I. Title.
   QC25.G658 2010
   530.078—dc22
                                          2008024880

Printed in the United States of America

10 9 8 7 6 5 4 3 2 1

To Our Readers: We have done our best to make sure all Internet Addresses in this book were active and appropriate when we went to press. However, the author and the publisher have no control over and assume no liability for the material available on those Internet sites or on other Web sites they may link to. Any comments or suggestions can be sent by e-mail to comments@enslow.com or to the address on the back cover.

♻ Enslow Publishers, Inc., is committed to printing our books on recycled paper. The paper in every book contains 10% to 30% post-consumer waste (PCW). The cover board on the outside of each book contains 100% PCW. Our goal is to do our part to help young people and the environment too!

Photo Credits: Shutterstock

Illustration Credits: All illustrations by Stephen F. Delisle, except Tom LaBaff, Figure 5.

Cover Illustration: Shutterstock

CONTENTS

Indicates experiments that are followed by Science Project Ideas.

INTRODUCTION

CAN YOU IMAGINE WHAT THE WORLD WOULD BE like today if wheels had never been invented? There would be no automobiles, no trains, no watches, no electric motors, no disk drives, no electric generators, no CDs or DVDs, no washing machines, no pulleys, no Ferris wheels, no wagons, and no motorcycles. There would be no roller or in-line skates, no skateboards, and no bicycles. And that is only a small part of the list. The wheel is probably the most important mechanical invention ever.

Why is the wheel so effective? How can its motion and that of objects on wheels be explained? The laws of physics can tell us. Physics is the science that deals with motion. This book will introduce you to those laws of physics that explain the motions of three very popular sports on wheels. The three are bicycling, skateboarding, and roller skating. These three sports are united because they all use wheels. They are also united by the fact that the wheels all depend on human muscle power. No motor turns the wheels and no animals carry or help push or pull the riders.

Thanks to the wheels, the riders in all three sports are able to travel long distances using their own muscle power.

They can glide along silently while enjoying the views around them. Moreover, the riders can make breathtaking turns on skates, launch themselves from skateboards high into the air, and race up a mountainous road on a bicycle.

Each of the chapters in this book contain experiments for you to do. The experiments are easy to carry out, use materials readily available, and help to clarify the laws of physics. Most experiments also include ideas for projects that you might do for a science fair.

HISTORY

Although wheels have been part of European and Asian civilizations for many centuries, the sports of roller skating, skateboarding, and bicycling appeared much more recently. Perhaps the earliest was the "skeeter," which appeared in Holland in the early 1700s. Ice skating in Holland was used to travel the numerous frozen waterways but was limited to the icy season. Some clever person invented dry-land skating for the summer by using wooden spools. He nailed the spools to strips of wood and attached them to his shoes. However, skeeters never got much use because of the muddy grounds and rough road surfaces in the summers.

Roller skating appeared next, followed by bicycling, as will be discussed later. The skateboard is the youngest of the three, having been around for a mere one hundred years.

SAFETY

Any use of wheels for sports can injure the rider if proper safety precautions are not taken. When engaged in experiments using a wheeled device, always wear the protective helmets developed for each. Also wear wrist protectors and knee and elbow pads for skateboards and skating. **When carrying out experiments where you ride on wheels, make sure a skilled adult is always present. Obtain the approval of a responsible adult before carrying out any of the science project ideas.** When you need to carry out an experiment on a sidewalk, avoid busy streets. For any experiment on a road, pick one where there is very little or no traffic and have someone present to warn you if a car is coming. Never do any of the wheeled sports when feeling tired, faint, or even slightly dizzy.

THE SCIENTIFIC METHOD

In carrying out the many experiments that are in this book, you will usually have an idea of what you expect to happen. That expectation, based upon your previous experience, is called a hypothesis. After you have completed the experiment, you will be able to conclude whether or not the hypothesis was supported by the evidence that you gathered. That is the nature of science—to develop hypotheses and to gather evidence showing whether or not a hypothesis is true. If, eventually, there is considerable evidence in favor of the hypothesis and none that contradicts it, the hypothesis is elevated to the level of a theory. The theory will probably suggest more hypotheses, which will require more experiments and so on and on, producing more and more scientific knowledge.

Scientists are always careful to keep dated records of their experiments. The records include information on what they did, the observations made, and the conclusion reached. As you carry out the experiments in this book, be sure to do the same.

With the help of this book, you can investigate what laws of nature make the use of a wheel so advantageous, why the use of wheels makes moving along much easier than just walking, how you can balance so as not to fall off the wheeled device, and many other aspects of the sports. Each of the three self-propelled wheeled sports will be examined in a separate chapter. The three sports are popular because they are such fun. Although each sport is very different from the others, they are united by the laws of physics and by the wheels on which they move. A chapter on wheels starts the book.

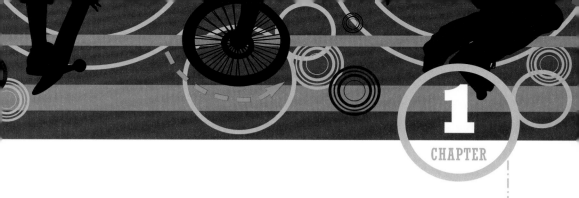

WHEELS

WHAT IS A WHEEL? A WHEEL IS A CIRCULAR device capable of rotating on a real axis. And what is an axis? An axis is a straight line, real or imaginary, passing through a body that rotates around the line. We all know that the earth rotates around a line through its center. That line is imaginary, not real. A wheel, however, always rotates around a real axis, such as

There has never been a visible wheel in the biological structure of a plant or animal on this planet. Although bacterial flagella, dung beetles, and tumbleweeds all use rotation for moving along, none has a real axis of rotation.

a round rod that passes through its middle from one side to the other.

The date of the appearance of the first operating wheel is shrouded in the mystery of the early times of human existence. The oldest single wheel found so far is a potter's wheel discovered in the region between the Tigris and Euphrates rivers (now Iraq). It dates back to about 3300 B.C. Wheeled vehicles may have quickly followed the discovery of the wheel. A wheel with spokes was first used for chariots in Egypt in about 2000 B.C.

The Romans produced a remarkable variety of wheeled vehicles. They built light, speedy chariots drawn by horses that were used for hunting animals, for sport, and for warfare. They also made farm carts with two wheels, four-wheeled wagons for heavy freight, and coaches for transportation of people. They built a network of roads for foot and wheeled travel that helped to unite the empire. Some of these roads are still used today.

EXPERIMENT **1.1**

Inventing the Wheel

MATERIALS
- heavy book
- flat tabletop
- 5 or 6 round pencils
- skateboard or quad roller skates (skates that have two pairs of wheels)

We will never know exactly why and how the wheel was invented. Those who study the distant past have accumulated some evidence to suggest one of the steps that might have led up to it. We can do a simple experiment that shows the idea that they have in mind.

1 Place a heavy book on a tabletop. Gently push the back of the book to move it in a straight line for about 30 cm (1 ft). Does the book slide easily? Did you have to keep pushing it the whole distance?

2 There is a way to get the book to slide more easily. You will need about five or six round pencils. Place them under the book lined up in a row as shown in Figure 1. Push the book as before. Is it easier or harder to push the book? What happens when the back pencils pop into the open, one by one? How can you keep the book moving easily?

A similar method is known to have been used in ancient times to move heavy objects. To do this, the workers put round logs under the heavy load. Then they pushed the load along the logs until the log at the back end came out from under. The front end of the load was now sticking out over empty space. The workers picked up the log that was free at the back and moved it to the front. The log was shoved under the front end and then the load was pushed further along. Each time that a log came free at the back end, it was moved up to the front and shoved under the front end. In that way, it was possible to move surprisingly heavy loads.

Moving logs forward from the back is, unfortunately, labor-intensive and time-consuming. This is where the unknown genius came in, the one who invented the great addition that converted a disk into a wheel. What was added to the disk?

The definition of a wheel given previously provides the answer. What was added was an axle. An axle (see Figure 2) is a spindle or shaft running through the center of the wheel. It rotates with the wheel. If you look at a roller skate or skateboard, you will see the axle that connects the two wheels. The axle turns in a sleeve that is screwed to the bottom of a board supporting the load. The axle eliminated the need to move

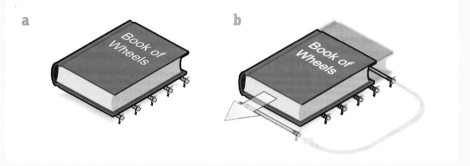

FIGURE 1.
a. A book on round pencils is pushed along. This is similar to the way a heavy load is pushed on logs.
b. When the front of the book is pushed past the front pencil, the back of the book moves past the last pencil. To continue rolling the book on the pencils, the exposed back pencil is moved up to the front and set under the book. The book can continue to be pushed easily as long as each exposed pencil in the back is moved up to the front and placed under the book.

FIGURE 2.
Two wheels are shown connected by an axle. Spokes run from the hub of the wheel to the rim. The axle has a support built onto it to carry the load. The load might be a covered wagon body, the bed of a truck or, perhaps, the body of a wheelbarrow. The load might require two wheels or four wheels, each pair connected by an axle. The axle is still free to rotate.

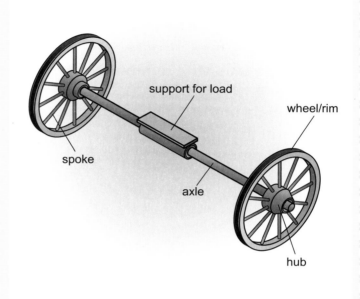

support for load

wheel/rim

spoke

axle

hub

logs back and forth and opened up the use of wheels for all the ages to come.

Why is pushing an object on wheels so much easier than doing the job without wheels? It is time for physics to help us find the answer.

EXPERIMENT **1.2**

Galileo and Newton's First Law

MATERIALS

- bowling lane with bumpers in the gutters or other location with level, smooth floor
- 6- to 9-lb bowling ball or substitute
- several thin books
- strong, smooth wooden plank about 90 to 120 cm (3 to 4 ft) long and at least 20 cm (8 in) wide
- pencil
- ruler

The earliest clue to why a wheel is so effective came in the sixteenth century from Galileo Galilei (1564–1642). Isaac Newton (1642–1720), born in the year that Galileo died and a great genius of classical physics, wrote, "If I have seen farther than other men, it is because I have stood on the shoulders of giants." He was referring to several brilliant men of science, but most specifically to Galileo.

Before Galileo, everyone believed that it was natural for a moving object to slow down until it stopped. This belief dated back 2,000 years to the natural philosophers, Aristotle and Ptolemy. Galileo boldly contradicted Aristotle, Ptolemy, and everybody else's beliefs. He said that objects would not come to a stop unless a force (a push or pull) slowed them down, nor would they start moving until a force pushed them into motion. Moreover, Galileo said that since moving objects all stopped sooner or later, there must be a force opposing the movement. The invisible force that opposes motion is called friction.

Galileo carried out several crucial experiments. One of

them used two inclined planks with smooth surfaces. He set them up in a V shape so that a metal sphere, when released at the top of one of them, rolled down one and up the other. However, the sphere never rolled back up to as high as the starting height. When Galileo made the surface of each plank smoother, the sphere rolled back closer to the height from which it started. Each time that he made the planks and the surface of the ball smoother, the ball rose a bit higher. Galileo drew the conclusion that if he could make the surfaces perfectly smooth, a perfectly round sphere would go all the way back up to the starting height. Since there was no way to make the planks or the ball perfectly smooth and the ball perfectly round, it could never happen.

In another experiment, Galileo lowered the second inclined plank (see Figure 3). The sphere still rolled up to almost the same height as it had initially, but it went a longer distance to do so. When Galileo lowered the second plank even more, the

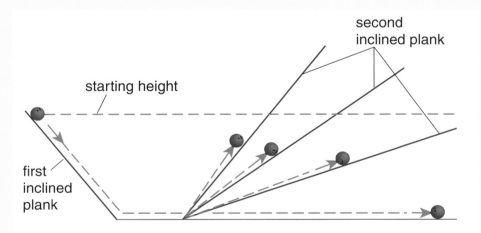

FIGURE 3.
The lower the second plank gets, the farther the ball rolls. However, each time the ball rolls the longer distance, it does not go quite as high as before. This is because the longer path develops more friction.

sphere still went to almost the same height as the second time, but it traveled an even longer distance to do so. After many variations of this, Galileo made a mental leap to the following conclusion: If he lowered the second plank until it was level, a perfect sphere rolling on a perfectly smooth road would roll on and on forever.

There is one place where you can observe what happens when an object moves along with very little friction. That place is a lane in a bowling alley that has been approved by the National Bowling Association. The lanes are constructed to be smooth and very level. They are also carefully oiled for most of the length of the lane. Each bowling ball is smoothly rounded except for the finger holes in the body.

At a bowling alley, obtain permission from the manager to carry out a science experiment where you will be rolling a bowling ball down a smooth wooden plank onto a lane. The wooden plank will be raised at one end and will control the speed of the ball. The board will not touch the alley itself. Request that bumpers be placed at both sides of the lane to keep the ball from going into the gutters.

If you do not have access to a bowling alley, you may use any smooth wooden or vinyl floor and a smooth, round, heavy ball. Perhaps your school has a gym or basketball court with a wood floor. Adjust the following instructions as needed.

1 Place one end of the plank on the floor at the foul line pointing down the middle of the lane.

2 Raise the back end of the plank on books so that it is about 10 cm (4 in) high. Use a pencil to place a mark about 15 cm (6 in) down from the top of the plank at about midway from either side.

3 Select a smooth bowling ball weighing 6 to 9 lb. Hold it at the mark (see Figure 4). Release the ball to roll down the plank onto the lane. What did you observe? Did the ball

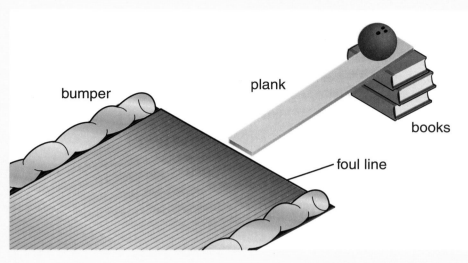

FIGURE 4.
A bowling ball is released at the top of a plank to roll down the plank onto a bowling lane. The plank has been raised 10 cm (4 in) at the back end by propping it up with a few thin hardcover books. Bumpers are placed in the gutters to prevent the ball from falling into them. The process is repeated from half as high and then from one-quarter as high. Does the ball make it to the end of the lane each time?

appear to speed up or slow down? Did it make it to the pins? Did it go in a straight line?

4 What do you think will happen if you lower the back end of the plank a little? Go ahead and drop the plank down to half as high as before. Roll the ball down it as before. What happens this time?

5 Do it one more time. This time, try it at one-fourth of the starting height. What do you observe?

Did you find that the ball, each time, kept slowly sliding all the way to the other end? If it veered toward one of the bumpers at the side, that was possibly because it rolled over a finger hole. Now you know why a bowling ball tossed by your little brother or sister still manages to make it to the end.

Newton built upon the ideas of earlier scientists by adding his own brilliant experiments, perceptions, and theories. From these came his Three Laws of Motion and the Law of Universal Gravitation. These laws are the foundation of classical physics. Newton's First Law, built upon Galileo's discoveries about motion, says that an object tends to stay the way it is. It keeps moving or it remains stationary unless a force acts upon it to change its motion. Newton's other laws of motion will be examined later in this book.

SCIENCE PROJECT IDEAS

- Predict the lowest height to which the board in Experiment 1.2 can be lifted and still have the bowling ball roll down the length of the alley. Test your prediction. Explain the result.

- Does the use of a heavier ball change the results obtained in Experiment 1.2? What about a lighter ball? Find out. Suggest a hypothesis to explain the results.

EXPERIMENT **1.3**

Friction

- heavy shoe with no heels or low heels
- smooth floor (vinyl or wood)
- sewing elastic 0.6 cm (¼ in) wide and at least 76 cm (30 in) long
- a partner
- measuring tape
- pen

Why does pushing or pulling a concrete block along the ground develop much more friction than when the block is on wheels? To find out, the force needed to move the concrete block when it is not on wheels needs to be considered first.

Scientists divide friction into two kinds: static and kinetic. Static friction (standing still) is measured by the force needed to get an object to start moving. Kinetic friction (sometimes called sliding friction) is the force needed to keep the object moving. This experiment will help show the difference between these two types of friction.

1 Tie one end of a long piece of sewing elastic to a heavy, flat-soled shoe. Put the shoe down on a smooth floor, such as a vinyl or wood floor.

2 Holding the other end of the elastic in your hand, extend the elastic horizontally to full length without stretching it. Have a partner measure the flat length from the tied end to where you are holding it at the free end. Your partner should place a mark with a pen on the elastic just where it meets your hand. Plan on holding the elastic at the same spot for the next steps.

3 Slowly pull until the shoe is just barely starting to move. With the help of your partner, measure the length of the extended elastic without further stretching it. Allow the elastic to gradually return to its unstretched length so that it does not snap against your fingers. The length of the stretched elastic is a measure of the force (push or pull) needed to start the shoe moving.

4 Repeat what you did, but this time continue pulling on the elastic until the object is moving at a slow but steady pace. Again, with the help of your partner, measure the length of the stretched elastic. As always, write your data into your notebook.

The force needed to get the shoe or any other object to start moving is called the static force. The force required to keep the shoe or any other object moving is a kinetic force. They are both frictional forces.

Now you can use the two measured lengths to compare the static force needed to start the shoe moving with the kinetic force needed to keep it moving. Are they the same or is one larger than the other? If so, which one?

You can expect to find that the force needed to get the shoe moving (static friction) is greater than the force needed to keep it moving (kinetic force). However, the difference in forces may be small. According to Newton's First Law, once the shoe has started to move, it should keep moving. Even the slightest force should keep it moving. That is, unless something pushes against it to slow it down. That something in our real world is friction. The kinetic force is needed only to overcome the friction. The actual size of the kinetic force depends on the causes of friction, such as the smoothness of the shoe's sole and the surface on which it is moving.

The force required to start sliding between two surfaces does not depend on the area of contact. This may seem quite surprising. When the famous physicist Charles Augustin de Coulomb (1736–1806) first made this known to the French Academy, they threw him out of the room. Those present all believed that the strength of the static frictional force depended on the area of contact. Experimentation showed that they were wrong.

Friction can be hindering but it can also be essential. Static force, for instance, is what holds things in place. Without it, they would start moving at the slightest touch. It anchors the furniture in your house. It holds us down so that a mild wind doesn't slide us away from where we are standing. It holds a pot on the stove, a ball on the floor, and a worker on a tilted roof. Friction is a force that opposes all motion—but without friction, we could not function. We would be sliding all over the place!

How the Wheel Works: Rolling Friction

Why is it so much easier to roll a vehicle on a road than to slide it along?

The reason is this: The wheel allows you to move one object across another one without sliding—that is, without kinetic friction. To see how this works, try this mini-experiment. Make a fist with one hand. Put the bottom edge of the palms of both hands together. Roll your fist up the palm of the other hand. Does your fist slide on your palm?

Your fist is acting like a wheel. It is not sliding at all. Each part that touches your other hand as you rotate the fist lifts right off it. There is static friction at the contact areas, but no friction from sliding. By eliminating the sliding friction, your fist acts like a wheel. In the same way, when a wheel rotates, a different patch of the rim keeps lowering to the ground. It touches the ground and then moves on and around. The contact patch does not slide along the ground at all; it only goes down and up. As a result, the contact that a wheel makes as it rolls along the ground is static, not kinetic (not sliding). Without sliding friction, it is much, much easier to move a load.

To use a wheel, you need to have some way to keep the wheel controlled, supporting a load, and rolling in the direction that you want. This is where the axle comes in. The two axles on a cart, for example, may be wooden poles. Each of the two ends of an axle passes through the middle of a wheel. The axles are attached to the body of the vehicle to support it. Examine a wheeled object, such as the roller skate or the skateboard that you will need for the next two chapters in this book. Find the axle. Notice how the shoe or board is supported on the axles. A toy car may also be examined to easily see the axles working.

Using a wheel and axle does not mean that all of the kinetic friction is eliminated. There is sliding friction in each wheel at the hub where the axle turns. If nothing were done about this, rapid motion might develop enough friction to heat up the hubs until they started smoking or even burning. To reduce friction at the hub, it helps to use slower motion, grease or oil to lubricate the hub, and a lighter load. A very effective way to reduce friction between the hub and the axle is to use ball bearings, which we will look at in Experiment 1.4.

SCIENCE PROJECT IDEAS

- Compare the force needed to keep a wheeled object sliding with the force needed to keep it rolling. Explain any difference.

- Use the sewing elastic method to investigate whether static friction increases with the weight of the object. What other properties of an object do you think could possibly affect static friction? Investigate those, too.

- Compare the static friction of a quad roller skate and a shoe and then of a quad roller skate and an in-line skate. For each pair, be sure to add weights, such as stones or marbles, to one of them as needed to keep the weights of the skate and the shoe the same. In advance, state your hypothesis for each.

- Compare the kinetic (sliding friction) of a quad roller skate and a shoe and then of a quad roller skate and an in-line skate.

- How does the roughness of a surface affect static friction? Consider a wooden surface. How is its static friction affected when it is sanded to become smoother? Find out by experimentation. Try some other surfaces. What conclusions can you make?

- What properties affect kinetic friction for a given material? How does the smoothness of the contact surface of the object affect friction? Consider the surface upon which the object slides. What other properties can you investigate? Find answers based on experimentation.

EXPERIMENT **1.4**

Bearings

MATERIALS
- 2 medium-sized paint cans with sealed covers
- 6 to 8 marbles
- tabletop

1 Set a sealed can of paint on a tabletop. Place another equal-sized can on top of it. Turn the top can around on the bottom can. Note how easy or difficult it feels to do this. Remove the top can.

2 Next, place six to eight marbles inside the rim of the bottom can, as shown in Figure 5a. The marbles will act as bearings. Put the second can on top of the marbles as in Figure 5b and turn the top can around. How did turning it feel this time? Compare the effort needed to turn the can with and without the marbles.

The marbles acted the same way that ball bearings do.

FIGURE 5.
a. Sealed paint can with marbles (ball bearings) in the groove of the paint can's cover.
b. Another can is placed on the marbles. Is it easier to turn the can when it rests on the marbles or when it sits directly on the cover of the paint can (no marbles)?

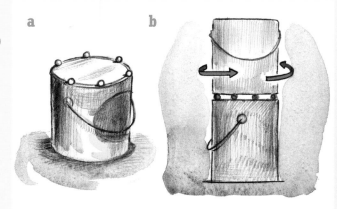

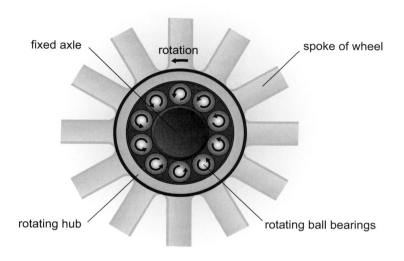

fixed axle

rotation

spoke of wheel

rotating hub

rotating ball bearings

FIGURE 6.
This is the central part of a wheel. Instead of the hub touching the axle, the hub touches the ball bearings, and the bearings touch the axle. It is this feature which reduces friction. The bearings at the bottom bear most of the load. As the wheel turns, bearings travel up and over the top of the axle. Then they move down the other side and back to the bottom again. The bearings constantly circulate. As a result, the bearings, the axle, and the wheel are subject only to static friction.

Figure 6 shows how ball bearings typically work when used in a wheel. As you can see from the diagram, the hub of the wheel doesn't actually touch the axle. The wheel touches the bearings that turn with the hub and the bearings touch the axle. The hub pushes up on the bearings and the bearings push up on the axle. The entire system—axle, bearings, and wheel—has static friction with only a little kinetic friction.

The causes of friction are partly, but not entirely, understood. Even though friction is so common, it is still a complex concept operating in many different ways. The term *friction* is really an umbrella term that covers many different aspects of the frictional force that opposes motion. Some of the characteristics of friction follow.

Surface roughness has a small effect on the frictional force. A soft surface, however, such as mud, can greatly increase it. A cracked or bumpy surface can also generate friction, especially when the wheel is small.

Particles coating one of the surfaces can make a big difference. A thin layer of grease can reduce friction to one-tenth of what it was. A little moisture can cut it by about 25 percent. A layer of grit will increase friction.

Where surfaces can attract each other by some form of chemical bonding, frictional forces can be strong. All surfaces on Earth have a layer of air on them which protects them from direct contact with other surfaces. If the surfaces are completely clean, flat, and free of air, they may actually stick tightly to each other. NASA found this out when a piece of metal stuck immovably to another one in an instrument on the Moon.

SCIENCE PROJECT IDEAS

- Compare static and kinetic friction for a square or rectangular block of wood on different surfaces, such as vinyl or smooth wooden floors, carpeting, sand paper, or a smooth floor with any of the following on it: oil, sandpaper, rice, sand, water, or a layer of marbles or ball bearings.

- Compare static and kinetic friction for a box when it is empty, when it is partly filled with stones, and when it is completely filled with stones. Repeat the measurements when the box is resting upon a layer of marbles.

- Bed races are fun competitions. They may be held at special student activity days in college towns or between different commercial organizations on national holidays such as July 4. The usual rules are that one individual sits in the bed while four others seize the four corners of the bed and push it along a designated route. Rules differ from one site to another. Some allow the bed to be reinforced, some allow special safety railings to be added, and some allow any structure made of rails and a mattress on four wheels to be used. Find a site that is planning a race. Offer your services to help design the bed to be used. Employ your scientific knowledge about wheels and friction to improve the structure of the bed. In your report, include the outcome of the race and suggestions for improving the bed in a future race.

SKATING ON WHEELS

TODAY THERE ARE TWO KINDS OF ROLLER skates, both popular. They each consist of shoes with wheels attached underneath. The quad has four wheels, one pair in the front and one pair in the back. The in-line skate has a shoe on four wheels (sometimes five) in a single line from front to rear. Figure 7 shows both. The two kinds of skates are equally useful for most purposes, but there are uses in which one has advantages over the other as will be examined later in this chapter.

The first recorded appearance of roller skates was in 1743 in a London stage performance. We don't know who the inventor was. The first patented roller skate was invented by M. Petitbled in 1819 in France. These early skates were

FIGURE 7.
a. A quad roller skate has a shoe mounted on the wheel frame to which two pairs of wheels are attached.
b. An in-line skate has a shoe mounted on a wheel frame, which has four or five wheels in a row from toe to heel.

In 1760 Joseph Merlin, a London instrument maker and inventor, made a pair of metal-wheeled boots. He decided to introduce them to the public at a masquerade party. Merlin wanted to make a grand entrance so he rolled in while playing a violin! The party took place in a huge ballroom lined with mirrors. As he approached a large mirror, Merlin realized that he could not brake himself. He crashed into the mirrored wall—violin, skates, and all. He survived, but the mirror, violin, and skates did not. The event was a topic of talk for many days—and roller skates were introduced to the public.

in-line designs, but they were not maneuverable. They could move only in straight lines or make very wide turns.

In 1863, in New York City, James Plimpton designed the first quad skates. They had a pivoting action that permitted the skater to move in a curve by leaning to one side. The skates were so successful that quad skates continued to dominate roller skating for more than one hundred years.

The biggest problem when learning how to roller skate is finding out how to stay up on them. How can a person on skates move ahead without falling? The short answer is "center of gravity."

By 1840, a beer tavern called the Corse Halle had opened near Berlin and had barmaids on roller skates serving beer. This was a practical solution that allowed the barmaids to quickly serve the many patrons in the huge tavern. The skating barmaids received much publicity and helped to popularize roller skating in Germany.

EXPERIMENT **2.1**

Center of Gravity and the Leaning Tower of Pisa

MATERIALS

- manila folder
- scissors
- strong thread
- metal washer
- pencil
- 3 straight pins
- board into which a pin can penetrate easily that is mounted vertically on a wall
- ruler
- tabletop that butts against a wall
- large book

In order to study what causes a roller skater, skateboarder, or bicyclist to fall, we start with Isaac Newton. He said that gravity pulls on an object as though all of its mass were concentrated in a single spot. That spot is the center of gravity, or COG, for the object. In a sphere where the mass is evenly distributed throughout, the COG is at the center of the sphere. For an object of irregular shape, the location depends on how the weight is distributed within that shape.

What does the COG have to do with falling? To find the answer to that, we are going to look at the Leaning Tower of Pisa. Why doesn't the Leaning Tower fall over? How much more can it lean before it does? How is it connected to a person falling on roller skates?

1 Start by cutting out a model of the Leaning Tower from an ordinary manila folder. Use Figure 8a as a guide. For this experiment, you will use Points A, B, and C as shown in the figure, but any three points could have been selected.

2 Mark Point A at the center top of the uppermost level of your model. At either side of the level below it, mark Points B and C. Your purpose in doing this is to find the center of gravity as described next.

3 Tie one end of a piece of thread about 35 cm (14 in) long to a metal washer. Tie the other end of the thread around a pin.

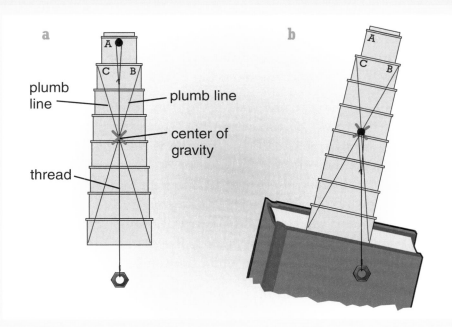

FIGURE 8.

a. A cardboard model of the Leaning Tower shows plumb lines drawn from points A, B, and C, meeting at the center of gravity.

b. The tower is leaning to one side. A plumb line from the COG does not go past the base of the tower, so it does not fall.

4 Push the pointed end of the pin through Point A. Using that pin, attach your tower model to a vertical board so that the tower hangs freely. The washer on its thread will be hanging right down the middle of the tower. A hanging line with a weight at the end (like your thread and washer) that points to the center of the earth is called a plumb line.

5 With a pencil and ruler, draw a straight line behind the thread of your plumb line. Remove the pin holding the tower and suspend the tower from Point B. Again draw a line on the tower under the plumb line.

6 Finally, repeat the process from Point C. You should have three lines drawn that cross over a single point as shown in Figure 8a. That point is the center of gravity of the tower. Mark it with an X. Push the pin with the plumb line hanging from it through the COG as shown in Figure 8b. Remove the tower and plumb line from the board.

7 Place a book next to the wall, upright on a table. Stand the base of the tower on top of the book with the plumb line hanging freely from its COG. Lean the tower lightly against the wall. To find out how far you can tilt the tower before it falls, start leaning the tower to one side by tilting the book sideways (see Figure 8b). Keep your eye on the plumb line and the base of the tower. Continue tilting the book until the tower falls. Where is the plumb line with respect to the tower's base when the tower falls?

You can expect to find that the Leaning Tower of Pisa falls over as soon as point X, its COG, moves past the base of the tower as shown by the plumb line. Now you know why the real Tower of Pisa is still standing. Its COG is still over its base. If the Tower should tilt even more, so that an imaginary plumb line from its COG passes its base, the Leaning Tower will fall over. Likewise, if you allow your own center of gravity to move vertically past your base of support when on a pair of roller skates, you will fall down. As long as the COG of any object is over its base, the object can lean without falling.

However, there is an exception to the above. A moving wheeled object, such as a skater, can lean into a turn without falling. Depending in part on the speed and angle of turn, the skater can do this when his COG is past his feet. This is because there is a combination of forces working in different directions—from the skater, the ground, and gravity. The combination of forces allows the leaning skater to go through the turn without falling, even though his COG is past the base of his feet—unless he goes too fast. The topic of leaning into a turn is complex. The full discussion that it merits is beyond the scope of this book.

SCIENCE PROJECT IDEA

Pick any three points on your manila model of the Leaning Tower of Pisa. Find its center of gravity by the same method as in Experiment 2.1. Pick another three points and repeat. Counting the result that you obtained in Experiment 2.1, compare the locations of the three COGs. If they aren't at the same spot, explain. Does this method have errors built into it beyond your control? If so, list them with a brief description. Which do you think is the biggest cause of error?

EXPERIMENT **2.2**

A Low Center of Gravity Helps

MATERIALS
- teenage boy
- teenage girl no taller than the boy
- wall
- low stool
- audience

The lower the center of gravity of an object, the more the object can lean or be leaned before it falls over. That is why designers concentrate the weight of automobiles, boats, and other moving structures as low as possible.

Following is an experiment that you can try with your friends. You need a boy and girl of about the same height.

1 Ask the boy and girl to stand up straight against a wall.

2 Place a low stool at the boy's feet. Tell your audience that you are going to ask the boy to pick up the stool without bending his knees. Then you will place the same stool at the girl's feet and ask her to pick it up without bending her knees. What do they think will happen in each case?

3 They will probably expect the boy to pick up the stool easily and the girl to also pick it up but maybe have a harder time of it. Ask the boy to pick up the stool without bending his knees. Then, ask the girl to do the same. What happens with each? Suggest an explanation.

The boy falls forward when he tries to pick up the stool as is shown in Figure 9. The girl picks up the stool easily without falling. The explanation has to do with the fact that most

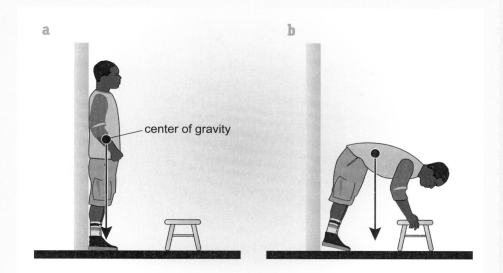

center of gravity

FIGURE 9.
a. This boy's center of gravity is at about the middle of his body when he is leaning against the wall.
b. When the boy leans over, his center of gravity goes past his feet and he falls over.

females have a lower center of gravity in proportion to their height than males do. When the male bends over trying to pick up the stool, his COG goes well past his feet. He cannot stay upright. The female, with a lower center of gravity, does not have this problem and easily picks up the stool.

The lower the center of gravity in an object, the more the object can lean before it falls over.

Here is a COG mini-experiment for you to try. What do you think will happen if you do the following? Stand with your left side firmly against a wall and your feet together. Then raise your right leg to one side. What happens? Suggest an explanation.

SCIENCE PROJECT IDEAS

- There are several different, simple methods for measuring the center of gravity of a person. They usually give an estimate at best. Find several methods and compare them. How well do they agree? Why are there differences in the results?

- Experiment 2.2 claims that a female has a lower center of gravity compared to height than a male does. Carry out an experiment to verify whether this is so.

- The validity of an experimental method of measurement states how close the method comes to obtaining the true value. Find several different methods of determining the COG of a human being. Examine how valid these are. For your purpose, you will need to be able to provide the true COG that you are measuring. Therefore, you need to construct some kind of model of the human body where you have distributed the weight so that you know the correct answer.

EXPERIMENT 2.3

How to Fall on Skates and Get Up Again

> **MATERIALS**
> - quad skates
> - smooth floor
> - wall
> - several beginning skaters

Practically everyone who has ever tried roller skating has fallen while learning. Having fallen, how does the skater safely get up again?

1 Suppose you are a skating teacher. How will you instruct your students to get up safely after falling? Work out steps for the student to take for this purpose. Test them out carefully yourself before teaching them.

2 List the steps to take in your notebook. How does the concept of the COG enter into this?

3 Now try your procedure out with several beginning skaters. How well does it work?

When falling on roller skates, experts suggest that a beginner should bend the knees as much as possible and try to fall onto one side. The larger the area of the body that hits the ground, the less is the force that hits any one spot of the body.

To get up after falling, experts advise the roller skater to get onto hands and knees. Keeping hands on the floor, one skate is placed outside of one hand. Then the other skate is placed outside of the other hand. The skater is now in a position to rise but must be sure to keep the COG vertically in line with the feet. This is a simple matter of staying as straight as possible, but it usually requires some practice.

How does your method compare to that of the experts? Which do you think is better? Why?

While good skaters may not be aware of it, they habitually maintain their COG in line so as not to extend vertically past their skates unless they are going into a curved path.

Braking With the Rubber Stop

Besides knowing how to fall and get up again, every skater must know how to stop. Unlike falling and getting up again, stopping on roller skates is very different from stopping on ice skates. Both quad skates and in-line skates have a rubber stop on the skate. One has it on the front of the skate. The other has it on the back. To stop or slow down rolling, just one rubber stop should be used. Right-handed individuals usually prefer to use the right stop, while lefties usually choose the left stop.

Try this mini-experiment.

1 Wearing your everyday shoes, stand up in the middle of a space on the floor. Imagine that you are wearing quad skates.

2 Lean forward as if you are skating. Place your right foot in back of you to slow down while you roll forward on the left skate. (Lefties, reverse this.) What did you do with your back foot?

You would probably push backward on the floor with the toe. When actually skating, you would push back and down with the toe stop on the front of your skate.

On both ice skates and roller skates, an axel is a move that starts by skating backwards into a leap. The skater makes one-and-a-half turns in the air followed by a graceful backward landing. When an axel is well-done, the skater appears to be defying gravity. Actually, gravity controls the leap. The leap upward slows as the skater ascends due to the downward pull of gravity. A point is reached where the upward movement has decreased to zero. Immediately, gravity starts to pull the skater down again, faster and faster. A champion skater lands gracefully in what looks like an effortless descent and continues to move smoothly backward on the surface.

Try the same thing again, but this time picture yourself wearing in-line skates. Lean forward as if you were skating. Place your right foot in front of you to slow down. What would you do with that front foot? Note that in-line skates are longer than quad skates.

The in-line skater would place the heel of the front foot on the ground in front, and would push forward and down to slow down and stop. When actually skating, there would be a stop on the back of that skate shoe.

Throughout the above processes the COG has to be pictured as centered over the skates.

Do you think that placing the stop at the back of the quad skate would work just as successfully as placing it at the front? Why or why not? Again, try it as if the skate were on your leg. What did you find out? What is your conclusion?

Imagine placing the rubber stop on the front toe of the in-line skates. Use the stop to slow down or stop the skate. What happens? Would it be a good idea to stop on in-line skates that way? Why?

SCIENCE PROJECT IDEAS

Be sure to wear a helmet whenever you wear skates. You should obtain the approval and supervision of a responsible adult, such as a teacher or parent, before you carry out any investigation.

- How much of an effect does wearing roller skates have on the COG of a body? Conduct an experiment to find out.

- Measure what happens to the center of gravity when a person does a deep knee bend. Explain. Does placing the feet further apart before doing the knee bend affect the result? Find out. Explain.

- Obtain a series of pictures of a side view of a skater moving rapidly on quad skates. Select at least five sequential frames showing the skater placing one leg and then the other forward while skating ahead. Make a copy of each of the selected frames on a copy machine. In each of these copies, place an X where you think the center of gravity of the skater is. Mark off the area on each showing how far the skater could lean forward or backward over his or her skates without falling. Use the method of Experiment 2.1. Explain your observations. Can a skater lean backward without falling? Will this be any different for in-line skates? Why?

- Test one or more ways that a skater might use to slow and stop quad skates besides a rubber stop. Show the methods with diagrams. Evaluate each method. Would it be any different for in-line skaters?

EXPERIMENT 2.4

The Third Law of Motion Applied With Roller Skates

MATERIALS
- 2 skaters on roller skates (quad or in-line)
- helmets
- about 1.5 m (5 ft) of strong cord

Isaac Newton's Three Laws are considered the basis for our understanding of force and motion in the visible world. Roller skates can be used to help us understand his Third Law. The Third Law states that every action has an equal and opposite reaction. When you walk, you push backward against the floor. The floor pushes back at you, moving you forward. If you could not push against the floor as in the case of slippery ice, it could not push back at you. Your leg would continue to go backward on the ice as you fell forward on your face.

Does the Third Law of Motion mean that if you lean against a wall, the wall is leaning on you? It certainly does. If the wall didn't push back at you when you leaned on it, you would push it down to the ground.

The Amish community in the United States uses in-line skating for transportation purposes, but not for recreation. The Amish still shun automobiles, electricity, and other modern technologies.

FIGURE 10.
Two skaters, A and B, are connected by a cord. Skater A pulls Skater B toward her. Newton's Third Law says that every action has an equal and opposite reaction. That is just what happens here. Skater A pulls Skater B toward herself, but Skater A is moved at the same time toward Skater B.

Skater A   Skater B

1 Two people on roller skates and wearing helmets should stand about 1.5 m (5 ft) apart. We'll call them Skater A and Skater B.

2 The skaters should hold opposite ends of the same cord. Note that if the skaters have a hard time staying upright, they can try bending their knees. This will lower their COG and make it easier to stay balanced. What do you predict will happen to Skater A when she pulls the cord inward toward herself? To Skater B? What actually happens? Explain.

When the cord is pulled inward by Skater A, Skater B is pulled toward Skater A. At the same time, Skater A is moved toward Skater B. This is shown in Figure 10, which shows Newton's Third Law in operation. A exerts a force on B. Therefore, B exerts a force on A. If A pulls hard enough, A and B might skate right past each other.

SCIENCE PROJECT IDEAS

Be sure to wear a helmet whenever you wear skates. You should obtain the approval and supervision of a responsible adult, such as a teacher or parent, before you carry out any investigation.

- Use roller skates to illustrate Newton's First Law of Motion other than the experiments done so far. Be sure that the examples you develop are safe for ordinary skaters to perform.

- Illustrate Newton's Third Law with skates using an example other than that given in this chapter.

EXPERIMENT **2.5**

Why Use In-Line Skates?

MATERIALS
- in-line skate
- quad skate
- 6 to 12 hardcover books of similar thicknesses

In-line skates have four or five wheels in a single row from front to back. This gives them a distinct advantage over quad skates when skating on pavement. Unlike the smooth floor of skating rinks, sidewalks have bumps and cracks in them. Quad skates roll into and out of the cracks—a bumpy process. In-line skates much more easily bridge sidewalk gaps so that the skater can easily roll long distances outdoors.

1 To see how the skates bridge gaps, construct a bumpy sidewalk out of at least six to twelve books placed in line with a short space between them (about 1 cm).

2 Move a quad skate from one side of this sidewalk model to the other.

3 Do the same with an in-line skate. How do they compare?

You will find that quad skates dip in and out of the spaces. In-line skate wheels follow each other so closely that they easily bridge the gap. Accordingly, when not skating on a smooth floor, it is better to use in-line skates rather than quads.

Group skating, mostly on in-line skates, is a popular social activity. During its height in the 1990s, there was a weekly Friday night skate party in Paris, France, that sometimes had as many as 35,000 skaters on a single night. Berlin, Frankfurt, Munich, Amsterdam, Buenos Aires, London, New York, and Tokyo all have had popular group skating, sometimes with as many as 10,000 skaters. An international group skate was held in 2007 in Tunisia. Halloween is a particularly popular group-skate night both in the United States and Europe.

EXPERIMENT **2.6**

Muscular Energy

MATERIALS
- watch with a second hand
- spring-loaded wooden clothespin
- a friend

To move on roller skates, a skater needs muscular energy.
The energy is supplied by a chemical in the muscles called ATP
(adenosine triphosphate). Although a muscle fiber contains only
enough ATP for a few twitches, more ATP is made as needed.
The body has three ways to do this. A small store of chemical in
the muscle can be easily converted to ATP. When that is used
up, another process takes over and glucose (sugar) is converted
to ATP. This process requires oxygen. Inhaling the needed
oxygen is what makes for deep breathing and panting when
exercising. With prolonged exercise, the muscles being used
may not be able to obtain oxygen quickly enough. Then the
body is forced to use glycogen stored in the muscle to make
ATP. One of the by-products of using stored glycogen is lactic
acid. Lactic acid is useless for immediate energy production. It
is what makes muscles sore after exercise. However, after the
exercise, the body uses lactic acid to remake glycogen. You can
feel for yourself what happens when the use of glycogen causes
the production of lactic acid in the muscles.

How long do you think you can open and close a spring-
loaded wooden clothespin (see Figure 11) between your
thumb and index finger before those muscles begin to tire?
How much longer do you think you can continue to do it?

1 Hold a spring-loaded wooden clothespin between your thumb and index finger. Count how many times you open and close the clothespin in one minute.

2 Don't stop when the minute is up, but count how many more times you open and close it during the second full minute. Don't try it a third minute—you can damage the muscle.

   Did you find that you scored much lower in the second minute? It is not because you are a weakling, but rather that the fast exercise you were doing had to use glycogen

Studies show that roller skating provides a complete aerobic (using oxygen from the air) workout. It involves the heart muscles and all of the body muscles. A study at the University of Massachusetts showed that in-line roller skating causes less than 50 percent of the impact shock to body joints that running does. Dr. Carl Foster of the University of Wisconsin Medical School has found that in-line skating as a form of exercise is as beneficial as running or cycling. Other studies have shown that roller skating is the same as jogging in terms of health benefits.

FIGURE 11.

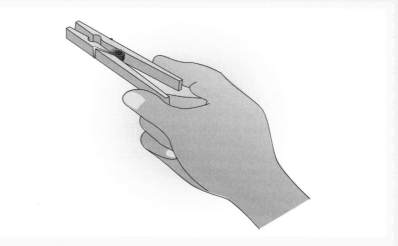

to replenish the ATP. The glycogen reaction produced lactic acid, which tired the muscle.

3 Allow yourself some time to recover. When your hand feels normal again, repeat the two minutes of clothespin exercise, but this time do it slowly. How did you feel this time after the two-minute workout? How did your score in the second minute compare to that in the first minute?

The expected result is that you will not get as tired as in the first part of this experiment. This slower exercise gave your muscles the needed oxygen to continue making ATP. How typical is your result? To find out, have a friend repeat the experiment with the clothespin. How do your friend's results compare with yours? What is your conclusion?

EXPERIMENT 2.7

The Law of Conservation of Angular Momentum

You have probably seen ice skaters or roller skaters spinning with their arms held gracefully outstretched. Then they bring their arms in close to their body with theirs arms crossed over their chests. Immediately, the skater starts spinning faster. Why does this happen?

To understand this rotation, you first need to learn about angular momentum. Angular momentum is equal to the mass of a rotating object multiplied by its velocity multiplied by the radius of the circle made by the rotating object. The equation for angular momentum is:

$$\text{angular momentum} = mvr$$

where velocity, v, stands for the angular speed.

Angular momentum stays constant as long as no outside force acts upon the system. Note that if we are dealing with the same object throughout, there is no change in mass. In that case, what must happen to the speed of the rotating object if the radius of motion (r) is increased?

The only way that the angular momentum can stay the same if the radius increases is for the velocity to decrease. A decreasing velocity means a slower rotation. Conversely, if the radius is decreased, then the same object will rotate faster.

When the skaters pull their arms inward, they are decreasing the radius of rotation. To conserve angular momentum, something else must become bigger. The mass of the skater cannot change, but the speed of rotation can and does.

You can try this for yourself without getting on skates or a skateboard. You will need a rotating chair for this, preferably one with arms.

1   Make sure you place the chair on a floor with plenty of free space around it.

2   Seat yourself on the chair holding two heavy objects in your lap such as 5-lb weights or heavy books (see Figure 12).

FIGURE 12.

A person sits on a rotating chair holding a heavy weight in each hand. Once the chair starts to rotate and is not touched after that, angular momentum does not change; it is conserved. When the weights are pulled inward (radius decreases), the rotation speeds up. When the weights are extended (radius increases), rotation slows down.

The Law of Conservation of Angular Momentum was discovered early in the history of physics. Johannes Kepler (1571–1630) was a brilliant, almost blind German mathematician who worked with the famous astronomer Tycho Brahe. It was when they were plotting the paths of the planets that Kepler worked out what later became known as the Law of Conservation of Angular Momentum. He was one of those upon whose work Newton built his famous discoveries.

You may put your feet on the base of the chair or hold them off the ground.

3 Holding the weights, extend your arms out fully from your sides. Make sure that you are seated securely.

4 Have an adult start the chair rotating. He or she should then immediately let go of the chair.

5 Now bring your arms slowly inward until they are hugging your body. Be careful. The chair may change speed rapidly. What happens?

6 Repeat the rotation, but this time reverse the motion of your arms by starting with your arms held close to your body and bringing them outward until they are fully extended. Does your result agree with the Law of Conservation of Angular Momentum?

You can expect to find that as you moved the weights inward, the chair rapidly sped up. When you moved your arms outward, the chair slowed rapidly, all in agreement with the conservation law.

As with all of the movements in roller skating, physics can explain what happens. There is much more that can be explored and understood in the science of roller skating, but we need to get on to the discussion of skating on skateboards, which comes next.

THE SKATEBOARD

SKATEBOARDERS LEAP OVER OBSTACLES, FLIP around in the air, make backward landings, and combine these and other tricks for many more amazing stunts. They seem to defy the natural laws of physics. How do they do it? Actually, it is the laws of physics that make such tricks possible.

A fundamental law of nature is the Law of Conservation of Energy. This says that the total energy of the system cannot be more or less than the system originally had. It assumes nothing from outside has been added or subtracted from the system. In other words, energy is conserved.

Within the system, however, energy can be moved around or converted from one form of energy to another. The law is well-illustrated by skateboarding in a half-pipe.

A half-pipe is usually formed out of planks closely fitted together to form a trough shaped like the bottom half of a U. A half-pipe may also be more like a half-circle as when a very large pipe is cut in half along its length. Often there is a flat section at the bottom of the half-pipe (see Figure 13). The depth of the full-size half-pipe is usually about 1.2 m (4 ft). The skater rolls on the skateboard down from the rim on one side of the half-pipe to the bottom and on up the other side toward its rim.

FIGURE 13. A HALF-PIPE

There are numerous shapes that may be called a half-pipe from a U to a half of a large pipe cut along its length. A flat section often appears between the two opposite rising sides. The flat section is longer for beginners and decreases greatly as skill increases. A rim is usually found at the top of each side of the half-pipe for the skater to stand on before going down the pipe. The horizontal length of the half-pipe varies but must be long enough to safely catch a skater who tumbles over.

EXPERIMENT **3.1**

The Law of Conservation of Energy

For this experiment, a metal wok will act as a miniature half-pipe.

1 Hold a glass marble at any point at the inside top of the wok. Release it. What happens when the marble is released?

2 Allow the marble to continue moving until it has just about stopped. When did the marble appear to be moving the fastest? Why did the marble keep rolling back and forth instead of just stopping at the lowest point in the half-pipe?

When the marble was released, it rolled down the wok and a good part of the way up the other side. Then it rolled down again and then back up, but not as high as the first time. Each time, the marble rolled along the same path, but not as high as before. (It is because the marble rolls in the same path each time that the wok can be substituted for a half-pipe.) The rolling of the marble demonstrates the conversion of one form of energy to another. When you lifted the marble to the top of the wok, you gave the marble energy simply because you lifted it against the downward force of gravity. The energy gained by the marble is called potential energy. It remains stored until the marble is released to roll downward. The source of the potential energy given to the marble comes from the chemical energy of the muscle action that you used to get the marble up there.

At the top of the wok, the marble has potential (stored) energy but no motion (kinetic) energy. When the marble is released, gravity immediately pulls it downward. As the marble rolls down from its high position, it is losing the potential energy it gained when placed at the top. Where does that energy go? The potential energy is transformed into kinetic energy. The lower the marble rolls, the less potential energy it has and the more motion energy it gains. This is shown by the fact that the marble speeds up as it descends the half-pipe. At the bottom of the pipe, the marble has none of the potential energy left that you gave to it. The potential energy has all been

The Law of Conservation of Energy, a fundamental law of classical physics, took a long time to become fully developed. Even though the first hint of the concept appeared in the early 1600s, it was not until 1843 that the full mathematical presentation was presented by James Prescott Joule. Only two years before that, an exposition of the concept by Julius R. Mayer was rejected by the scientists at the meeting where he presented his paper.

converted to motion energy. At that point, the marble reaches its greatest speed. The slope of the rest of the half-pipe forces the moving marble up again.

But the marble does not roll all the way back to the top. Why? It is converting motion energy to potential energy as it rises higher in the half-pipe. The motion energy should have been just enough to get it back to the starting height. Where did it lose the energy needed to roll all the way back up to the top? The Law of Conservation of Energy says that the energy cannot be destroyed, but it can be converted to another form of energy. The missing energy must have been changed into some other form. What was the other form?

Did you say that friction did it? You are right. The energy of motion was transformed into heat energy due to friction. The friction arose largely from contact between the surfaces of the glass marble and the wok. Most of that was due to tiny imperfections in those surfaces. Some bouncing and sliding occurred as a result. Although heat was developed, you probably could not feel the wok heating up. That is because a marble is small, so the heat it developed was small. The wok is much larger and spreads heat quickly because it is made of metal. The small quantity of heat that was developed quickly spread around the wok. The wok could not warm up enough for you to detect it. Note that a little kinetic energy was transformed into sound energy (you could hear the marble rolling).

SCIENCE PROJECT IDEAS

Be sure to wear a helmet whenever you ride a skateboard. You should obtain the approval and supervision of a responsible adult, such as a teacher or parent, before you carry out any investigation.

- As in Experiment 3.1, try rolling a marble down wide, shallow bowls made out of different materials, such as wood, china, plastic, or handmade ceramic. How do they compare? What can you conclude?

- What difference does it make if the bowl has a flat bottom instead of a rounded bottom?

- Try rolling other balls approximately the same size as the marble, such as wooden, plastic, rubber, and steel balls, and plastic beads. Use the same bowl or wok for all of them. Allow the balls to roll down the bowl or wok. What conclusions can you reach? Carry out further experiments based on what you have found out so far.

- Make several miniature half-pipes of the same width but with different depths. You can make them out of half of a manila folder bent to a U shape that stays in place. Does the depth make any observable difference when the same ball is rolled down the half-pipes? Hypothesize an explanation.

- Find the height above the bottom when a skater rolls down a half-pipe and the height to which the skater rolls up again on a simple pass. Using the data, you can estimate the percent of energy lost to friction. The percent equals the height back up again divided by the height from which the skater started multiplied by 100. Find a way to carry out such an investigation on a real half-pipe and take the needed measurements to calculate the frictional effect. Compare your prediction with the results from measurements.

SCIENCE PROJECT IDEAS

- Investigate the materials used for the surface of half-pipes in various indoor rinks. Explain the advantages and disadvantages of each material. Which of the materials, based on the previous Science Project Idea, would be best for skateboarding? Why?

- Compare results when rolling a marble down different surfaces held securely on the surface of a miniature half-pipe. You can make the half-pipe out of a manila folder (see above). Besides the surface of the manila folder itself, consider covering it smoothly with wax paper, plastic wrap, sandpaper, and smooth aluminum foil. Which surface develops the most friction, and which develops the least? Hypothesize explanations.

- You can make a device to represent, to a very limited extent, a small person on a real skateboard by putting weights into a strong cardboard box on a skateboard. A box that is 23 cm (9 in) wide by 30.5 cm (12 in) deep and whatever length you can find is adequate. For weights, you can use books, bricks, or other weights firmly set inside the box. Cushion the box with a thin sheet of foam rubber to help protect the half-pipe. Balance the box carefully upon the skateboard, or upon two skateboards, and secure it firmly. Carry out your experiments at an indoor skateboarding facility. Take all appropriate precautions. Get the approval of the manager of the facility before you start. Devise experiments such that your device can help answer questions about skateboarding. For example, what happens if an overlay of appropriate tape is placed on the wheels of a skateboard so that the wheels are roughened slightly? What if they are made smoother or larger?

EXPERIMENT **3.2**

Unweighting

> **MATERIALS**
> - bathroom scale with a dial (Digital scales will not work for this.)

A skilled skateboarder can roll down a half-pipe and roll back up to the other rim of the half-pipe. The skateboarder may even twist up into the air and land on the half-pipe at about the height from which he started the roll. According to Experiment 3.1, he should not have enough energy to get all the way back to the starting height. Has the Law of Conservation of Energy been violated? Never! Experiment 3.2 will shed some light on how a skater gets all the way back up.

First, would you believe that you can change the weight of your body momentarily just by bending your knees? Try the following.

1 Stand on a bathroom scale that has a dial on it. Notice what your weight is.

2 Watching the scale, suddenly lower yourself by bending your knees. What happens to your weight as you bend?

According to the scale, you lost weight for a moment as you bent your knees. Your upper body lost the support of the lower body in that instant and hung there, momentarily weightless. Consequently, the scale showed your weight falling. What happened is called unweighting.

Will this work in reverse?

3 Watching the scale, quickly stand erect after having bent your knees. Does the same unweighting occur or is it different this time?

This time, your weight went up for a moment. You were raising your COG. Momentarily, you appeared to gain weight.

Unweighting uses the same principle as pumping on a swing. To pump yourself upward on a swing, you first raise your legs at the bottom of the swing. You momentarily fling them up even higher at the top of the swing. Then you lower your legs as the swing starts to descend. When you raised your legs, you raised the body's center of gravity. Lifting the center of gravity gives you additional potential energy. Having flung your legs as high as you can, you lower them as gravity starts to pull you down again. On the way down, your potential energy is transformed into kinetic energy. Pumping enables you to keep swinging higher and higher.

Skateboarders pump in a half-pipe by first dropping to a crouch near the bottom. Then, when entering the rising part of the half-pipe, the skaters straighten up. This allows them to change their center of gravity and gain enough energy to get back up higher than before. If done correctly, skateboarders can get all the way back to the top of the ramp and even twist into the air above it. Next time you watch skateboarders performing in a half-pipe, note how their posture depends on where on the half-pipe they are.

Tony Hawk is a highly accomplished skateboarder. Videos showing Tony Hawk on a half-pipe make it look as if he is defying the Law of Conservation of Energy as he reaches higher and higher on each pass on the half-pipe. However, we know that he is providing the extra energy from his own muscular effort by using a pumping action to increase the height of his center of gravity.

Skiers and snowboarders also unweight themselves by bending their knees. You may have done it too, even if you do not participate in those sports. If you have ever accidentally stepped on a sharp object while barefoot, you probably bent your knee and dropped your hip as you shifted your weight to the other foot. You unweighted the foot that was hurting.

SCIENCE PROJECT IDEAS

Be sure to wear a helmet whenever you ride a skateboard. You should obtain the approval and supervision of a responsible adult such as a teacher or parent before you carry out any investigation.

• Make a visual record with a camera or other device to show what happens when a person unweights on a bathroom scale with a dial. Explain what happens at each step. Relate this to the energy change that occurs during pumping.

• Make a visual record with a camera or other device to show how a skilled skateboarder changes position while on a half-pipe to gain energy of motion. For the first pass, the skateboarder should descend once, bend all the way down at the bottom, roll up the half-pipe and leap onto the rim. On the second pass, the skateboarder should bend partway, rolling back down if the rim cannot be reached. The third time, the skateboarder should not bend at all. Indicate changes in potential and kinetic energies. Compare energies lost and gained. Provide conclusions and explanations.

• Predict what will happen if a skateboarder pumps near the top of a half-pipe. Will this be a safe maneuver? Why? How can you safely test your prediction?

The Ollie

MATERIALS

- wooden board about 2 cm thick by 25 cm wide by 60 cm long (¾ by 10 by 24 in)
- carpeted floor
- wooden broom handle (not plastic) at least 35 cm (14 in) long

The ollie is a fundamental skateboarding motion and the basis for many skateboarding tricks. The basic form was invented in the late 1970s by Alan "Ollie" Gelfand. In its simplest form, it is a way of jumping around on a skateboard that allows skaters to hop over obstacles and off and onto sidewalks. It leads to many more complicated tricks. What is most astonishing about an ollie is that the skateboard appears to stick to the skater's feet even in midair. People may think that the skateboard is attached to the skater's shoes, but it isn't. Skateboard tricks may give the illusion that the laws of physics are being disregarded, but the truth is the exact opposite. The laws of physics explain what happens during the ollie maneuver. The explanation is complicated, so the following provides only a start to understanding the ollie.

1 Place a broom handle on a carpeted floor.

2 Set the middle of a board across the handle so that the long part of the board is perpendicular (at right angles) to the broom handle.

3 Slide the board along the top of the broom handle until the length of the handle beneath it is about 15 cm (6 in) from the end of the board.

FIGURE 14.

By shifting weight on a board balanced on a broomstick, the basic idea of how weight is shifted on a skateboard to get one end of it to leap up can be examined. This is the movement that begins the ollie, the basis of many of the stunts in skateboarding.

4 Stand on top of the board. Move so that your right foot is near the short end of the board (see Figure 14). Place your left foot about 45 cm (18 in) away from the short end. The broom handle is now acting like a pivot under the board. The board should not be able to roll from its position when stepped on.

5 Shift a little to place most of your weight on your left foot. What happens on the right side of the board?

6 Shift enough to place most of your weight on your right foot. What happens on the left side of the board?

7 Crouch down at the beginning and repeat these both rapidly as you stand up.

The ollie involves, in part, shifting one's weight on the skateboard so as to make one end of it go down while the other end goes up. It uses the principle of a lever, as does your board and broom handle. A lever can make a small force larger, as you did when you stepped on the right side of the board. You made the force even larger when you crouched down and then rapidly stood up.

FIGURE 15.

a. In performing an ollie, the skater first crouches down, then accelerates himself upward by quickly straightening his legs and raising his arms. **b.** The rear foot exerts a large force on the tail of the board causing the board to pivot counterclockwise. It pivots around the rear wheel. This causes the board to bounce up and pivot clockwise around its center of mass. The board and skater are now in the air. The skater slides his foot forward on the rough surface of the board to drag the board higher yet. **c.** Now the skater starts to level out as does the board. If the skater times his motions correctly, his feet seem stuck to the board. Still seeming to touch the board, the skater and board begin to fall. **d.** As they land, the skater bends his legs to lessen the impact.

Although the most talented skaters perform what seem to be unbelievable tricks on the board, they could not do them without the superb equipment that scientific investigations have provided. The entire board is carefully engineered. Nothing equals laminated sugar maple wood for the skateboard. Many other materials have been tried—for example, epoxy, fiberglass, and carbon-loaded nylon—but none has the toughness, feel, and response of the sugar maple wood.

The skater stamps down on the rear of the skateboard so as to cause the board to leap up off the ground.

The skater needs to crouch down to begin an ollie because jumping high requires a low center of gravity. To test this, stand on the ground and try to jump up without crouching down. How high could you get? Does crouching down lower enable you to jump up higher?

Here is a shortened description of how a skater gets into the air, as shown in Figure 15. While speeding forward on the skateboard, the skater shifts his weight onto the foot at the far back of the board. Then he crouches down. He leaps upward, raising his arms and straightening his legs. As he does, he stamps hard on the very back end of the skateboard. By stamping down hard, the front end of the board lifts up. The skateboard, unlike the plank in your experiment, has a back end that tilts upward. When the skater stamps down hard, not only does the front end lift, but the board also pivots counter-clockwise on its back wheels. Now the back end of the board hits the ground hard. The ground pushes hard back on it. This causes the board to bound up and also to pivot in the opposite direction. The whole board moves up into the air. So does the skater.

Skateboards have a grip tape on them, which helps the skater grip the board with his shoes. Just after the skateboard leaps into the air, the skateboarder drags his front foot forward and up on the grip tape so as to drag the board even higher. Now the skater begins to level out the board by pushing the front leg down. This raises the rear wheels. If the skater times this motion correctly, the skater's back foot and the back of the board rise together, appearing to be stuck together. Both skater and board soon start falling due to gravity and they do it together. As the board touches ground, the skater's knees bend to absorb the force of impact.

Twisting and turning in the air involves the Law of Conservation of Angular Momentum (see Chapter 2), as will be observed in the next experiment.

In August 2006, Aaron Fotheringham, just fifteen years old, accomplished an historic first. Confined to a wheelchair since birth, he became the first person in the world to do a successful back flip somersault in a wheelchair going down a ramp.

SCIENCE PROJECT IDEAS

Be sure to wear a helmet whenever you ride a skateboard. You should obtain the approval and supervision of a responsible adult, such as a teacher or parent, before you carry out any investigation.

- Observe a skilled skateboarder hopping off a sidewalk onto a road and hopping back on the sidewalk again on the other side. Does the skateboard appear to stick to the skater's feet? Take high-speed photographs of the leap and see if you can find a space between the skateboard and the skater. Repeat with another skater. What do you conclude? You can extend this idea by following other stunts where the skateboard appears to stick to the skater's feet while going into the air and down again.

- Take slow-motion photography of a skateboarder doing an ollie at the moment when the skateboarder strikes the back end of the skateboard to leap into the air, and then when the skateboard pivots and then pivots in the opposite direction. Establish the sequence of events. Show where and how Newton's Laws apply to this.

EXPERIMENT **3.4**

Turning in Midair

MATERIALS
- a partner (optional)
- trampoline (optional)

An admirable leap on the half-pipe is to make a pass from one side to the other side and finish with a twist up into the air at the end of the pass. The skater ends up on the slope ready to swoop back to the other side. This is called a frontside 180. However, a frontside 180 seems to violate the Law of Conservation of Angular Momentum (see Experiment 2.7). The problem in this case is that the skater is rotating in the air above the half-pipe. No force acts upon the skater while in the air except gravity. Gravity pulls the skater down, not around. The skater is isolated from any other outside force. From where is the force coming that twists the skater into the air?

The explanation involves a surprising source for the force.

1 Stand in an open space facing a partner.

2 Now jump high up. As soon as you are in the air, your partner should point either to your right or to your left. You must immediately turn your legs in the pointed direction. You may have to try this midair turn several times before you can accomplish it. Doing this on a trampoline gives you more time to carry it out. If you don't have a partner, just decide as soon as you have jumped which way to turn. Be sure not to decide in advance of jumping or you may push off already turning. What did you have to do in midair to rotate?

What you had to do in order to turn in midair was to rotate

your arms and torso in the opposite direction to your legs. The rotation of your torso canceled the rotation of your legs. Presto! You managed to turn in midair without violating conservation of angular momentum.

Watch as a skater turns in midair or view it on a recording. You should be able to see the motion of the arms and torso compared to that of the legs.

SCIENCE PROJECT IDEAS

Be sure to wear a helmet whenever you ride a skateboard. You should obtain the approval and supervision of a responsible adult, such as a teacher or parent, before you carry out any investigation.

- Skateboards are made in different shapes and lengths. Investigate the advantages and disadvantages of one or more of these. Devise tests to check them and carry out the tests. Also consider interviewing experienced skaters to find their opinions of the properties of different models.

- Investigate advanced tricks that can be done on a skateboard and explain with illustrations and text the physics involved that make one or more of these particular tricks possible.

THE BICYCLE

YOU ARE PUSHING SO HARD ON THE BICYCLE pedals to get up the hill that your muscles are starting to burn. At last, you are at the top and you can see all around you, below and above. You shift your weight forward as you begin to coast downhill. The bike speeds up so you need to concentrate, but you are enjoying the speedy descent. When you come to level ground, you are able to coast much of the way. Several times you stop and dismount as you see something interesting along the road. Then you mount the bicycle again and take off. A bicycle can be one of the most pleasing types of transportation, allowing you to easily do things not possible in a car.

A bicycle is also more energy-saving than any other common mode of transportation. It uses much less energy than walking, for example, to cover the same distance. In fact, it has been calculated that you will use less energy to

The bicycle is closely connected to the invention of the first successful airplane. The Wright brothers were avid bicycle riders and bicycle mechanics. Early on in their exploration of flight, they used to ride in the street with wing parts attached to the bicycle to find out how the wings behaved in the wind. Selling bicycles helped to provide the money to invent the plane. Bicycle parts were used in the first plane, with bicycle gears and chains to turn the plane's propellers.

go a certain distance when bicycling than when on a horse, on a moped, in an auto with five riders (and even much less with only one rider), and on a train with many riders, all traveling at typical speeds.

Figure 16 on the next page shows the parts of today's bicycle.

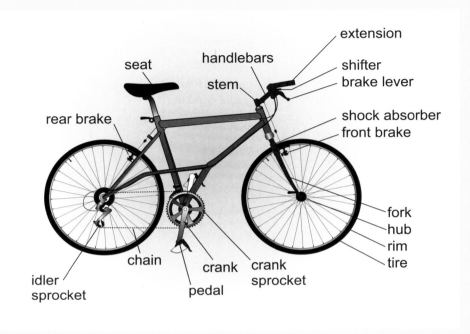

FIGURE 16.

John Lennon, one of the Beatles, said, "As a kid I had a dream—I wanted to own my own bicycle. When I got the bike I must have been the happiest boy in Liverpool, maybe in the world. Most kids left their bikes in the backyard at night. Not me. I insisted on taking mine indoors, and the first night I even kept it by my bed."

EXPERIMENT **4.1**

How to Balance a Bicycle

> **MATERIALS**
> - bicycle
> - helmet
> - thin, round, straight stick at least 60 cm (24 in) long
> - smooth and level section of dry pavement
> - pail of water
> - knee pads, elbow pads (optional)

When you are riding smoothly ahead on a bicycle, what keeps you from tipping over to one side? Every beginning cyclist falls over a number of times before being able to keep the bicycle erect. What is the secret?

To understand what happens, first consider how you balance a stick on your palm.

1 Balance a thin, round, straight stick upright in your palm. What motions are you making to keep the stick upright? Repeat the process as needed to come up with an answer.

To balance the stick, you keep moving your hand. If the top of the stick starts to fall to the right, you move your hand to the right. This moves the bottom of the stick back underneath the top and returns the stick's COG to over its base. You even move it a bit extra to the right to make the stick tilt back to the left a bit. This means that you have to move your hand left to again regain balance so that your hand heads back toward where you started. Of course, the stick goes right on tilting so you go right on moving your palm back under the tip again to balance it.

How is this connected to a two-wheeler? To get a clue, you

can observe the tracks that a bicycle makes as it moves in a straight line.

1   First find a smooth paved sidewalk or a smooth asphalt or cement tennis court or running track.

2   Pour a pailful of water on the ground (you can omit this step if you can find a puddle of water on an otherwise dry pavement).

3   Put on your helmet and get on the bike. You may also choose to wear knee pads and elbow pads.

4   Ride through the wet pavement and straight onwards for at least 4.5 m (about 5 yd). What can you tell from the bicycle tracks? You may need to throw more than one pail of water down before you can get a good set of wet tracks.

You can expect to find that the tracks do not show really straight line motion. Instead, they show that the bicycle weaves a bit from side to side as it travels ahead. It seems that to ride the two-wheeler, you have to carry out the same type of maneuver that you did when you balanced the stick. If the bicycle starts to tilt to the right, you steer right. This gets the wheels (and the bicycle's COG) underneath you again. Similarly, when you turn too much to the right, you have to steer left to balance the bike. You end up repeating a series of mini-turns left and right to keep from falling as you continue ahead. The mini-turns are so small that you are not ordinarily aware of them as you cycle, but the bicycle tracks show them.

Can you keep a bicycle from falling over when it is stationary?

Put your helmet on. Sit on a bicycle and try to keep it upright in place. Are you able to do it? If so, how did you manage it?

An especially skilled cyclist might be able to keep a stationary bicycle erect, but most riders cannot do it for long, if at all.

About ten thousand people in the United States cycle from coast to coast every year. Usually, they go from west to east to get past the Rocky Mountains early in the trip. After that, the winds blowing at their backs on the Great Plains make cycling easier. The first coast-to-coast rider was Thomas Stevens in 1884. He took 103 days to ride about 5,600 km (3,500 miles). He went from Oakland, California, to Boston, Massachusetts. Today such a trip takes about fifty days, shorter mostly because of well-paved roads.

You can't steer to the right or left to quickly recover as you did with a moving body. Instead, you have to try to tilt your body over to get the bicycle to tilt back to where it was. This, however, creates instability since the bicycle may tilt past its center of gravity. The answer to the question is that, unless you are a very skilled rider, you should not expect to keep a stationary bicycle from falling over.

SCIENCE PROJECT IDEAS

Be sure to wear a helmet whenever you ride on a bicycle.

• Tires on bicycles range from narrow to wide. Which kind, if any, show more side-to-side weaving when you ride the bicycle in a straight line? Why?

• Which does more weaving, a bicycle moving slowly or one that speeds along in an apparently straight line? Explain.

• If you can prevent a bicycle from weaving, will you be able to ride it forward? Suggestion: You can set up a path between two boards so that it is only wide enough to allow the two-wheeler to move without any side-to-side weaving.

• Test a unicycle to find out if it is balanced when moving in an apparently straight line by weaving side to side.

• Wheel sizes range from those small enough for children on up to 66 cm (26 in) for taller adults. Does a smaller wheel size result in less weaving?

• Can you alter the center of gravity of a standing bicycle to make it more stable when standing still? Do it and test how well the method works.

EXPERIMENT **4.2**

Turning a Bicycle Compared to Turning a Tricycle

> **MATERIALS**
> - bicycle
> - rider with helmet
> - tricycle
> - smooth and level section of pavement
> - pail of water
> - pen or pencil
> - different rider with helmet for tricycle (optional)

1 Put on your helmet and get on a bicycle.

2 Ride it at a fairly rapid pace on a smooth and level pavement, such as a concrete or asphalt tennis court.

3 Smoothly make a right turn as if going around a corner and continue a short distance. Write down what you did to make the turn. You may repeat the turn as often as needed to be able to write your description.

The scientists at the Exploratorium in San Francisco, California, have pointed out that it is much easier to make a turn on a bicycle than to explain it. The process is complex. Not only is the bicycle's position important, but also the rider's position and the position of the front wheel.

If you stayed upright on a bicycle without leaning while going around a corner, then you were probably moving the bicycle through a series of small straight lines. Each small line changed the direction a little in order to make the curve. Use the wet method of Experiment 4.1 to find out if this was so.

You may have instead made the turn by leaning it in the same direction that you were going. If you did the latter, you would automatically start your turn just when the bicycle was falling to the side that you wanted to turn.

4 Now get on a tricycle. If you cannot fit on an available tricycle because it is too small for you, enlist the help of a smaller person, preferably someone in the same grade that you are. Ask the tricycle rider to ride a short distance and then to turn the bike to the right. A tricycle rider usually turns the tricycle by turning the handlebars in little straight segments. Together, the short turns cause the wheels to move in a curve. However, the tricycle can also be turned by leaning to one side provided that the rider is going slowly. First the rider should turn the tricycle by leaning to one side. If the tricycle does not tilt when turned, the rider repeats the turn but does it a little faster this time. This is repeated, speeding up gradually each time until the tricycle starts to tilt a bit as it moves into the right turn. Why did the tricycle tilt at a higher speed?

Ordinarily, three-wheeled cycles are much more stable than two. Unlike a bicycle, there is no trouble balancing a tricycle when it is stationary, with or without a rider. However, when a tricycle is leaned into a curve, the cycle may easily tilt past its center of gravity and crash. This is especially likely when the tricycle is going fast. Because a tricycle is limited in speed this way, the two-wheeler is much more popular even if not as stable.

SCIENCE PROJECT IDEAS

Be sure to wear a helmet when riding on a bicycle or tricycle.

• Construct a display that shows why a stationary tricycle does not easily tip over.

• Use the method of wet tracks from Experiment 4.1 to find out what happens when you turn a tricycle around a corner. When do changes in speed make a difference? Why? Be careful not to allow the tricycle to tilt more than a little.

• How does a cyclist riding "no hands" steer the bicycle? How does the "no hands" bicyclist get around a corner? Find out and show evidence of what you saw.

EXPERIMENT **4.3**

How Do Bicycle Gears Work?

All the bicycles sold these days are advertised as three-speed, ten-speed, or some other numbered speed. What are they talking about and what do the speeds accomplish?

If you have ever huffed and puffed your way up a hill on a bicycle, you know what the different speeds are referring to. They refer to the fact that you can change the distance that the bike travels in one full rotation of its pedals. The gears on the bike are what control the distance traveled. If you have to push the bicycle a long distance up a hill with each full rotation of a pedal, you will really have to exert a large force on that pedal. It is hard work. By changing the gears, you can push the bicycle a shorter distance for the same rotation of the pedal. You won't have to work as hard each time, so it will help to make the climb manageable. Each different gear is said to give the bicycle a different speed.

The following experiment will show you the idea behind a gear.

1 Place a short wooden board on a flat work table.

2 **With adult supervision,** hammer a nail into the board about 10 cm (4 in) from the left side and midway between the sides.

3 Set another finishing nail about 10 cm (4 in) from the right side.

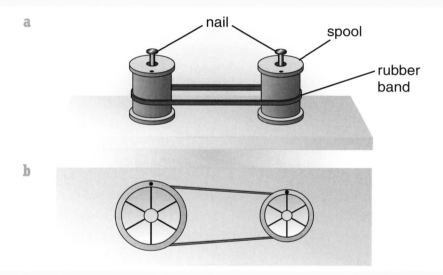

FIGURE 17.
a. When two spools have the same size radius, turning one spool transfers the motion to the other one by means of the rubber band. Each part or whole rotation of one spool produces the same rotation in the other one.
b. When the spools are different sizes, the ratio of the circumferences determines how far one spool turns when the other has turned a complete rotation. If the larger spool has a circumference twice that of the smaller one, every time the larger spool rotates once, the smaller one will rotate twice. Similarly, one gear can cause another one to turn five times as fast or maybe one-fifth as fast or any other ratio needed.

Although cycling on a two-wheeler was immensely popular with men in the 1890s, it was frowned upon for women. Nonetheless, women shortened their skirts and weighted the hems so that they would not fly up and went right ahead cycling. Their success in what had been an exclusively male sport resulted in greatly encouraging the women to try to overthrow another exclusively male right: the right to vote.

4   Select two spools of equal size and set one on each nail.

5   Select a rubber band so that it has to stretch to connect the two spools together as shown in Figure 17a. The rubber band should be tight enough to turn the spools together but loose enough so that they can be turned easily.

6   Make a heavy dot on the top of each spool with your pen or pencil. Use the dot to tell you how much the spool turns.

7   Now turn one spool exactly one full rotation. How much does the other spool turn? Turn the other spool one full rotation. How much does the first one turn?

8   Replace one of the spools with a larger one as shown in Figure 17b.

Does using a low gear or a high gear require more energy to ride a bicycle uphill? In low gear, you push the pedal down fewer times, go a long distance for each one complete rotation of the pedal, but must push hard each time. In high gear, you push the pedal down many times, go a short distance for one complete rotation of the pedal, but find it much easier to push the pedal each time. Professor Stephen Fitzgerald of Oberlin College worked the question at the beginning of this paragraph into an experiment for his students. Their results show that the two pathways use the same quantity of energy. A few turns of the pedal that move the bicycle a long way each time adds up to the same energy as many turns of the pedal that move the bicycle a short way each time.

9 Turn the larger spool one full rotation. How much does the smaller one turn?

10 Finally, lift the rubber band off one of the spools. Shape it into a figure eight and slip it back over the spool. What happens when you turn the larger one now?

When you rotated one of the two same-size spools, the

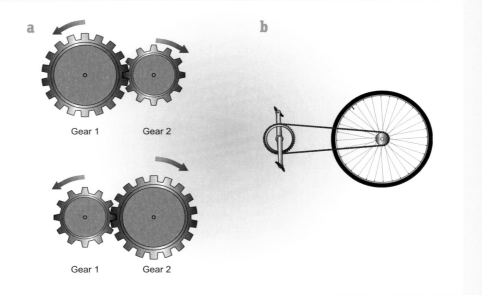

Gear 1   Gear 2

Gear 1   Gear 2

a   b

FIGURE 18.

a. Gears can have teeth on one that fit into the teeth on the other. As a result, when when one turns, so does the other. In the gears shown, they rotate in opposite directions. One gear is large and the other is small. As a result, every time that the small gear makes one complete rotation, the larger one makes less than a full rotation. When the large gear makes a full rotation, the small one makes more than one rotation. By counting the teeth, the ratio of the number of rotations for each can be calculated.

b. A chain can be used to connect two gears (sprockets) with teeth so that one turns the other.

rubber band transferred the motion to the other one so that it rotated the same distance in the same direction. When the spools were different in size and the larger one was turned one rotation, the smaller one made more than one rotation. If the smaller one had been turned one full rotation, what would have happened to the larger one? Try it if you are not sure of the answer. When the rubber band is twisted into a figure eight, turning the first spool causes the other one to rotate just as much but in the opposite direction to the first one.

Gears with teeth can directly turn each other when the teeth of one slip in and out of openings in the other as shown in Figure 18a. Gears can also indirectly turn each other when they each have teeth and are connected by a chain into which the teeth of each can slip. This is shown in Figure 18b. The invention of the gear chain for a bicycle made a big difference in bicycle structure because the rider no longer had to sit over the pedals attached to the wheel. The rider could sit in the middle of the bicycle where the center of gravity was more easily managed. Turning the pedals would then move the chain to transfer the motion to the rear gear similarly to the way the rubber bands did to the spools. A system has also been developed whereby gears can be interchanged at each wheel. At this point, you may wish to turn over your bicycle and study how one gear affects the motion of another. Also check the mechanism that moves the gears to find out which is high gear and which is low gear.

SCIENCE PROJECT IDEAS

Be sure to wear a helmet whenever you ride on a bicycle. You should obtain the approval and supervision of a responsible adult, such as a teacher or parent, before you carry out any investigation.

- Invent a Rube Goldberg system using only gears and gear chains.

- Historically, the first wheels developed were solid. Modern improvements include spokes to make them lighter. What is the advantage to lighter wheels? Invent another way to make wheels lighter and find out how effective it is.

- According to Newton's First Law, when you ride a bicycle, both you and the bicycle are going in the same direction at the same speed. If the bicycle is braked sharply, it will stop but you may not. In that case, you will fly over the front of the bicycle. Should a cyclist wear a seat belt? Investigate reasons for and against and state a conclusion.

EXPERIMENT 4.4

Air Is Everywhere Around Us

> **MATERIALS**
> - 2 identical sheets of paper (8½ in by 11 in)

Although we are often unaware of it, air is always present in the space around us and exerts a force on everything it touches. A quick experiment can demonstrate this to you.

1 Take a sheet of paper and crumple it up into a ball.

2 Hold the ball up high and allow it to drop to the ground while you observe the fall.

3 Next take another sheet of paper of the same size and hold that one up high as before. Let go of it and allow it to drop to the ground. What differences do you observe in the falls of the sheets of paper when balled up and when uncrumpled? How do you explain it?

The crumpled sheet of paper falls straight down. The uncrumpled sheet floats down, sailing around a bit as it does. It is the air that makes the difference. The very rapidly moving molecules of air batter at the surface of the sheets of falling paper. Since the uncrumpled sheet has much more surface, the molecules of air have a large target to keep striking. They slow down its fall compared to the ball of paper.

A bicycle encounters friction from the axle, the chain, and the tires rolling along on the ground. However, the major force that slows a cyclist down is the air. The greater the speed of the bicycle, the greater the air drag. A cyclist traveling on a level road at 16 kph (10 mph) uses 50 percent of his or her power against air drag. When the speed goes over 40 kph (25 mph), as much as 90 percent of the cyclist's power is needed to overcome air drag. It has been calculated that to go one mile on a bike requires pushing aside three thousand pounds of air. The currents of moving air in any wind add another level to this. Wind coming from 80 degrees to the left or right directly behind the cyclist is a good wind that helps the rider. However, wind coming from any other direction slows the cycle down (see Figure 19).

While a bicycle can be streamlined to minimize air resistance, up to 70 percent of the air drag on a moving bicycle is due to the body surface of the cyclist. Lance Armstrong, perhaps the most famous racing cyclist of all time, wears a specially designed helmet to decrease air resistance. It permits air to flow over his head and smoothly down his back. Most racing cyclists wear drag-reducing clothing. To minimize air drag, the posture of the rider is by far the major factor.

FIGURE 19.

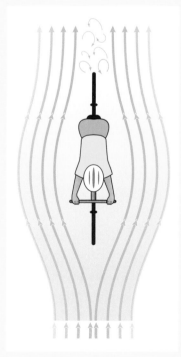

In this diagram, the wind is being pushed aside as a cyclist pedals through it. The lines with arrows indicate the direction of the air flow. As the wind passes the cyclist, the rider's body blocks some of it. This resistance to the wind builds up air pressure in the front of the cyclist and reduces it in back. The air in back forms whorls and curls as it fills the space that the cyclist has cleared. The result of all this is that wind coming in front of the cyclist acts as a brake on the bicycle. Any change in posture or clothing that can help reduce the resistance is of great importance in competitive or long-distance cycling. Note that while air coming toward the rider from in front slows the cycle down, wind moving toward the cycle from in back speeds it up. Still, only part of the wind coming from the back (80 degrees back left around to 80 degrees back right) can help the rider.

Riding Posture on a Bicycle and How It Affects the Bicycle Speed

When a body interferes with the air as it moves forward on the bicycle, the air creates air pressure upon the body. Along with the frontal pressure, there is a temporary low vacuum in back of the rider as air rushes in to fill the space left by the rider moving ahead. The higher pressure in front acts to push the cyclist backward at the same time that the cyclist is straining to pedal forward. Different positions of the body lead to better body streamlining by decreasing air resistance. An upright position creates the most air resistance. The more the cyclist can hunch over into a streamlined position, the less the air resistance. By using handlebars that curl under and forward, the crouched position is easier to achieve. The hunched posture is often used, but results in backaches for many cyclists. A position almost parallel to the ground produces the least air resistance. However, it is not only difficult to maintain, it is also dangerous. The reverse of that is the recumbent position. On a recumbent bicycle, the rider is leaning backward in a more or less cradled position. A streamlined recumbent bicycle that is enclosed can cut off seven-eighths of the air drag. Every record for bicycle speed on land is held by a rider on a recumbent machine.

SCIENCE PROJECT IDEAS

Be sure to wear a helmet whenever you ride on a bicycle. You should obtain the approval and supervision of a responsible adult, such as a teacher or parent, before you carry out any investigation.

- Design and carry out an experiment to test air drag for different positions of a rider when cycling.

- Test the time needed for each of a set of falling objects from two or more heights and compare air drag. Explain how your results are connected to bicycling.

- Improve the design for the current bicycle helmet so as to decrease drag while maintaining safety. Note: For safety, it is important to be able to get one finger under the helmet and two fingers below the strap. Test the improved design. Suggestion: To substitute for a human head, a soft melon such as a cantaloupe could be considered. Compare your design to the current helmet in use.

- What are the properties that make a difference between the ordinary bicycle and the recumbent machine with respect to air drag? Investigate to find out how much of an advantage the recumbent bicycle has. Does the recumbent bicycle have disadvantages or other advantages compared to ordinary bicycles?

EXPERIMENT **4.5**
Drafting

MATERIALS
- **an adult**
- candle
- candle holder
- matches
- pie plate

Drafting is often used in bicycle races. The cyclists bunch up as they ride in a pack known in the famous Tour de France race as the peloton. The front cyclist, who bears the brunt of the wind, shelters the cyclist in back from the wind. The cyclists behind the front one can save as much as 40 percent of their cycling energy by having their air resistance reduced. The maneuver is most effective when the cyclist is within a few inches of the cycle in front of him. If you have ever seen birds flying in a V formation, they are drafting. Each bird takes a turn at leading the V. To get an idea of how drafting works, try the following.

This experiment shows how drafting works by observing the effect of shielding an object from the wind. The wind strength and direction will be shown by the use of a flame on a candle.

1 Place a candle in a candle holder.

2 **Have an adult** light the candle with a match, and then extinguish the match safely.

3 Holding the candle in front of you in your right hand, slowly turn yourself in a circle to the left. Observe what happens to the flame. In what direction does it move?

4 Repeat as before, but this time also hold a pie plate in your left hand about 45 cm (1½ ft) left of the candle.

Charley "Mile-a-Minute" Murphy was a well-known bicycle racer who accomplished the feat celebrated by his nickname in 1899. He rode behind a large windscreen mounted on a train moving in front of him. Workmen for the Long Island Railroad had laid 5 km (3 miles) of entirely smooth and level track using carefully joined wooden planks. Murphy cycled furiously behind the train and rammed it at the end. He was grabbed and hauled aboard the train just before the planked course ended. He was still clutching the bicycle between his legs. The bicycle tires were charred and burning at that point. In 1995, Fred Rompelberg rode 268.66 kilometers per hour (166.94 mph) on the Bonneville Salt Flats. He rode behind a racing car with a big windscreen.

5 Again slowly turn in a circle to the left while keeping the pie plate the same distance left of the candle. Which way does the flame turn this time?

6 Repeat this once more, but this time keep the pie plate 10 cm (4 in) to the left of the candle the entire time. As you rotate, in what direction does the flame move this time?

As you made your first turn to the left just with the candle, the flame moved to the right. With a pie plate at 45 cm from the candle, the flame still moved right. However, when you shortened the pie plate distance to 10 cm, the flame moved left along with the pie plate.

The cause of the difference was the air in the form of a wake behind the pie plate. The air that passed around the pie plate was disturbed as it did so, but by the time is was 45 cm away, it had smoothed out again. Close to the pie plate, however, the air in the wake caught the candle and moved the flame in the same direction as the plate.

Aerodynamics plays a big role in the movement of a bicycle. As with the candle flame, the front cyclist in a peloton produces a wake immediately in back with the air moving in the same direction as the cyclist. The cyclist immediately in back is close enough to the lead rider (several inches) to get pushed along in the same direction, saving much energy. A cyclist who is further away may not get this advantage but is still partially shielded from air drag.

Self-powered vehicles are fascinating in the way that human capabilities make use of wheels for almost magical achievements in transportation. In this book, you have been introduced to some of the interesting and often unusual properties of self-powered vehicles and the explanations that scientists have for them. Enjoy your further explorations of self-propelled vehicles on wheels.

SCIENCE PROJECT IDEAS

Be sure to wear a helmet whenever you ride on a bicycle. You should obtain the approval and supervision of a responsible adult, such as a teacher or parent, before you carry out any investigation.

- Investigate and estimate how much advantage in saved energy is obtained by a rider in a peloton directly in back of the leader. How is the time that the leader usually remains in place dependent upon the speed or on the slope of a hill?

- An enclosed, streamlined regular bicycle (the rider sits leaning forward) has been built and tested. Compare the test results to those for an enclosed recumbent bicycle. Perhaps you can suggest improvements in the design of the enclosed regular bicycle.

- How can the center of gravity of a bicycle be changed? Try one way of doing it and observe the effects. For example, does changing the center of gravity of a bicycle affect its speed downhill?

- Compare and analyze the bicycle coasting distances obtained with any of the following:
  - lower tire pressures versus higher tire pressures
  - wider tires versus narrower ones
  - going downhill with knobby tires versus smoother tires
  - going on level roads with knobby tires versus smoother tires
- Also compare and analyze the ease and speed of turning a corner with each of the four properties listed: tire pressure, tire width, and two situations for tire smoothness.

GLOSSARY

air drag—The opposition by air to motion through it.

air resistance—*See* air drag.

axis—The center line around which something spins.

ball bearings—Small metal spheres in a space between the axis and hub of a wheel.

center of gravity—The point within a body where all the mass can be considered to concentrate.

drafting—An object moving close behind another one to minimize air resistance.

energy—The capacity to do work.

friction—An invisible force that opposes forward motion.

gear—A disk on an axle that engages another one in order to change the latter's speed or direction of motion.

half-pipe—A smooth, wooden structure with a U-shape or similar shape used by skateboarders.

hypothesis—A tentative explanation of a physical occurrence.

in-line skates—Roller skates with four or five wheels in a line from front to back.

kinetic friction—A force opposing forward motion of a moving body.

potential energy—Stored energy in an object due to its position.

quad skates—Roller skates with two pairs of wheels.

recumbent bicycle—A bicycle in which the rider is seated leaning backward in a cradled position.

revolve—To move in a circle or loop around a central point.

rolling friction—A force opposing rolling motion.

rotate—To spin around a real or imaginary axis.

speed—The distance traveled by an object per unit of time.

static friction—A force opposing initial forward motion of a stationary body.

streamlined—Shaped to minimize drag.

theory—A logical explanation of events that occur in nature that is supported by all evidence.

unweighting—Changing weight by suddenly bending the knees.

velocity—The speed and direction of motion of an object.

wheel—A circular device rotating around a real axis.

FURTHER READING

Books

Gardner, Robert. **Bicycle Science Projects: Physics on Wheels**. Berkeley Heights, N.J.: Enslow Publishers, Inc., 2004.

Gardner, Robert. **Ace Your Sports Science Projects**. Berkeley Heights, N.J.: Enslow Publishers, Inc., 2010.

Glass, Susan. **Prove It!: The Scientific Method in Action**. Chicago: Heinemann Library, 2007.

Haduch, Bill. **Go Fly a Bike! The Ultimate Book about Bicycle Fun, Freedom and Science**. New York: Dutton Children's Books, 2004.

Invisible Force: The Quest to Define the Laws of Motion. Washington, D.C.: National Geographic, 2006.

Levine, Shar, and Leslie Johnstone. **Sports Science**. New York: Sterling Pub., 2006.

Wiese, Jim. *Ancient Science: **40 Time-Traveling, World-Exploring, History-Making Activities for Kids***. Hoboken, N.J.: John Wiley, 2003.

———. **Sports Science: 40 Goal-Scoring, High-Flying, Medal-Winning Experiments for Kids**. New York: John Wiley & Sons, Inc., 2002.

Internet Addresses

Exploratorium. Sport Science. <http://www.exploratorium. edu/sports/index.html>

The Physics of Bicycling. <http://physicsofbicycling. homestead.com/>

USA Roller Sports. <http://www.usarollersports. org/>

INDEX